Write it Out!

An anthology of LGBTQ+ writing from Ceredigion and Carmarthenshire

Published by Cowry Publishing
Gwisgo Ltd, 8 Sgwâr Alban, Aberaeron,
Ceredigion, SA46 0AD Wales, UK

www.cowrypublishing.co.uk

First published in December 2019

The right of The Writers to be identified as the authors of this work has been asserted by them in accordance with the Copyright, Designs and Patents Act of 1988.
Copyright The Writers ©2019.
Printed and bound in Ceredigion by Gomer Press
Cover design: Paul Raven, Emma Lloyd
& Karen Gemma Brewer

A CIP catalogue record for this book is
available from the British Library

ISBN 978-1-908146-03-8

All rights reserved. No part of this publication may be reproduced, stored in a retrieval system or transmitted in any form or by any means, electronic, mechanical, photocopying, recording or otherwise without the prior written permission of the publishers. This book may not be lent, hired out, resold or otherwise disposed of by way of trade in any form of binding or cover other than that in which it is published, without the prior consent of the publishers.

Acknowledgements

Crewyd y gweithiau yn y llyfryn hwn yng ngweithdai ysgrifennu creadigol prosiect Write it Out a oedd yn rhan o Gynllun Nawdd Llên er Lles, Llenyddiaeth Cymru.

The works in this booklet were produced in the Write it Out creative writing workshops which was part of Literature Wales' Literature and Wellbeing Funding Scheme.

All profits from the sale of this booklet will be donated to Galop, the LGBT+ anti-violence charity.
Registered Charity: 1077384   www.galop.org.uk

Contents

6	Rhagymadrodd	gan Lleucu Siencyn
7	Foreword	by Lleucu Siencyn
8	Introduction	by Helen Sandler
9	Editorial	by Karen Gemma Brewer
10	The Writers	by The Writers
13	Ruth Fowler	Death of the Author
14		Misogyny at the Movies
17	Kate Gallon	Blackthorn
22		Gofod
23		Growing
25		Gwerful Mechain's Genitals
27		Home
29	Annabelle May Hampton	Blonde or Brunette?
30		Blonde or Brunette
31		Coincidence
32		Identity
33		Life But Not As I Know It
34		My First Dress
56		This is Your Vagina
37		Towards An End
38	Nic Herriot	Show and Tell
43	Maj Ikle	Pretending to Protest
50		Two-Thousand-Eighteen
51		Vagitus

Contents

53	Mair Jones	Honour
55		Balchder a Bysedd
56		Ode To All That Is Woman
58	Matthew Woolfall Jones	Pulse
60	Emma Lloyd	Mystery Shopper
67		Sin Girls
68	Martagon	Boil Wash
69	Carole Powell	Difficult Windows
71		how things are
72		smoke-rings
73		Through the Glass
74	Paul Raven	A Void …..
75		Growing Tomatoes
76		Waiting & Watching
78	Ren Williams	Gravitate
82		Mewling Quim
83		The Proper Biological Terms

Rhagymadrodd

Mae'n bleser gan Llenyddiaeth Cymru lunio ychydig eiriau i gyflwyno'r casgliad hwn sy'n deillio o weithdai ysgrifennu creadigol yn Aberystwyth gyda Helen Sandler ac yng Nhaerfyrddin gyda Karen Gemma Brewer. Roedd y gweithdai yn archwilio lleisiau'r gymuned LGBT mewn awyrgylch ddiogel, gan ddatblygu mynegiant creadigol, a chynyddu hunanhyder a hunan-werth.

Drwy ein Cynllun Nawdd Llên er Lles y derbyniwyd cefnogaeth ar gyfer y gweithdai. Mae'r cynllun yn cynnig cymorth ariannol a hyfforddiant i awduron ac artistiaid i ddyfeisio a chyflawni cyfres o weithdai ysgrifennu creadigol gwreiddiol yn y gymuned. Caiff pob prosiect ei ddyfeisio gan awdur neu artist gyda grŵp arbennig mewn golwg.

Cyfranogiad mewn llenyddiaeth yw un o brif flaenoriaethau Llenyddiaeth Cymru a gellir dysgu mwy am ein gwaith a'n Cynllun Strategol ar gyfer 2019-2022 ar ein gwefan.

Mae gan bob un ohonom ein straeon i'w hadrodd, ond nid pawb sy'n cael yr un cyfle i wneud hynny. Mae'r cynllun hwn yn agor y drws i lenyddiaeth i grwpiau ym mhob rhan o Gymru, gan roi'r cyfle iddynt brofi nodweddion llesol y ffurf gelfyddydol hynod hon.

Lleucu Siencyn
Prif Weithredwr, Llenyddiaeth Cymru

Foreword

It's my pleasure to introduce this collection of writing which is the result of creative workshops in Aberystwyth led by Helen Sandler and Carmarthen led by Karen Gemma Brewer. These workshops safely explored the voices of the LGBT community, encouraging creative expression and increasing engagement and confidence.

The workshops received funding through Literature Wales's Literature for Wellbeing Funding Scheme, which offers financial support and training for writers and artists to create and deliver original community-based creative writing projects, devised with a specific group in mind.

Participation in literature is one of our key priorities, as is promoting the health and wellbeing of individuals. You can learn more about the work of Literature Wales in our Strategic Plan for 2019-2022 on our website.

We all have stories to tell, but not everyone is offered the same opportunities to do so. This scheme opens the door to giving groups and individuals the opportunity to explore the benefits of this remarkable, democratic art form.

Lleucu Siencyn
CEO, Literature Wales

Introduction

It has been a real pleasure to lead the Write It Out! creative writing project in Aberystwyth, funded by Literature Wales. The group met every Tuesday evening for six weeks in spring 2018 to explore different forms of writing. Some were already experienced writers, while others produced their first creative writing at the workshops. It was a supportive group full of original voices.

Around the same time, Karen Gemma Brewer was running a similar project further south, and some of her group came up to Aberystwyth in May 2018 for a fabulous joint reading at Aberration, the LGBT+ arts night. It was wonderful to see how well the authors read and how their work spoke to the audience.

I'd like to thank Mared Roberts of Literature Wales and Debra Croft of Aberystwyth University for their support for the workshops. We're pleased to have this anthology as a permanent record of the project and we hope you enjoy reading it. Some of the Aber group have continued to meet and help each other with their work, and I'm sure we can look forward to reading more from all of these exciting writers in the future.

Helen Sandler
Project leader, Aberystwyth

Editorial

Prose and poetry from an LGBTQ+ perspective - finding out, coming out, getting 'caught' yes, but also - life, love, loss and the rest of it. Two groups, one in Aberystwyth, one in Carmarthen, experienced writers rubbing shoulders with first timers, post-teen to pre-pension, all unified by a common motive to take up their pen and write.

What a read they have delivered! The work in here is imaginative, informative and exciting, editing has been a joy requiring the lightest of touches and the content is as relevant to the straight reader as to the LGBTQ+ community.

But this project is not only about the writing. In our tandem groups Helen Sandler and I have seen participants grow in confidence, some releasing their work to the public for the first time, others taking their first steps before a live audience. With many maintaining contact through various spin-off groups and activities, Write it Out lives on.

I am thankful to Literature Wales for their support and the opportunity to be part of this project; Mared Roberts for her guiding hand throughout and much needed assistance with the Welsh language elements of this anthology; co-project leader Helen Sandler for her input to the anthology and organising a fabulous performance night in Aberystwyth; Emma Lloyd for the Write it Out logo; and Paul Raven for his cover image, input to the design and supply of cake.

Enjoy the read and expect to see these names again.

Karen Gemma Brewer
Editor
Project leader, Carmarthen

The Writers

Ruth Fowler – by day Ruth works as an Equalities Officer in the Human Resources Department at Aberystwyth University, by night she co-organises Queer events called Aberration. Ruth enjoys writing to escape from life's daily stresses.

Kate Gallon has a background in avant-garde poetics and queer live art, loves grey areas and is a nicer person to be around when writing regularly. Note to self.

Annabelle May Hampton is a 60-year-old cleaner, artist and post-op transwoman with a BA and MA Fine Art and little interest in financial gain, finding greater satisfaction in creating visually or with the written word.

Making sense of life through her art, which together with her trans-identity has always been with her, she sees her writing as an extension of the same process. Never sure what she is writing about or painting until she instinctively feels it is finished and can then make sense of it and read or look at it with clear eyes.

Nic Herriot has spent most of her years writing short stories and generally making things up. Coming out as Lesbian in her thirties only enhanced her life and she thoroughly loves who she is now.

As she entered her 40's a bank loan enabled Nic to do a Masters in Creative Writing at Trinity College Carmarthen. It must have worked as she has had several stories published as well as discovering a love of performing flash fiction on stage. Nic happily plagiarises her family's adventures and overheard conversations on public transport for ideas.

Maj Ikle is a proud dykewriter living off-grid in a handmade house as part of a community in rural west Wales. Winner of 2014 Asian Cha magazine competition with the poem *the City Park*. Her story *Loser* was published in Glitterwolf June 2014.

Her alter ego, Jane Campbell, made her directing debut with a short film *Avocados Are Not The Only Fruit* with support from Iris Prize Outreach and is currently writing and seeking publishers for her memoirs *The Dyke*, about surviving Tories and homophobia in 1980's London.
http://majikle.blogspot.co.uk/

Mair Jones is an aspiring writer and historian who completed an MA dissertation on the Queer History of Wales in Aberystwyth. In her spare time, she sleeps, usually beneath many cats, tries to read and write, listens to Welsh and Queer music, volunteers, and occasionally writes a blog. She is proud to have co-written the script of an Iris Community Film made in Aberystwyth. @mairsaysno

Matthew Woolfall Jones is a writer who doesn't write much. But seeing as this makes as much sense as using a colander for a coffee cup, he's jumped at the chance to put pen to paper and make something. Sometimes hilarious, sometimes heart-breaking, this course has given Matthew the perfect space to create something. He's looking forward to seeing his name in print before he turns 30, for the right reasons.

The poem 'Pulse.' is dedicated to the LGBT+ communities in Florida and in south Wales.

Emma Lloyd moved to Aberystwyth nearly sixteen years ago to study Creative Writing at the University, and somehow never left. She's a passionate mental health activist, and is the creator and host of the podcast Me and My Brain. She likes mammoths, volcanoes, and squeezing as many pop culture references as possible into her work.
www.emmalloyd.co

Carole Powell often finds inspiration in the moving landscapes of driving and walking, and many of her poems are begun while parked or perched in odd places.

Other influences are dance and movement practices, photography and other art forms. There is a curiosity to discover how to integrate these in new ways.

Paul Raven normally behind the counter at Tea Traders in Carmarthen, the specialist tea shop he runs with partner Nick, describes himself as an inexperienced and reluctant writer more comfortable brewing tea than composing fiction.

Having relocated from Flintshire in 2017, this project enabled him to meet other members of the local LGBTQ+ community and gave him the encouragement to try creative writing for the first time, finding the experience enjoyable, rewarding and surprisingly liberating.

Ren Williams is the pen name for Bread, a weird and important poet and geek who lives on the edge of nowhere in Wales. They also write little stories, creative non-fiction and blogs. They also sleep a lot – this may or may not be related.

Death of the Author
by Ruth Fowler

I praise the shape of
the woman's body –
God did not once
gift her shoddy.

What wizardry is
her tongue and breast!
Without her, life
has no zest.

Is this writing
an homage to she,
or is it just
misogyny?

With reference to
cunt, flaps and curtain,
I cannot truly
say I'm certain.

If God is the father
according to you,
then I doubly
doubt you too.

Does your gender
change my perception?
Or are you just
a historical conception?

Misogyny at the Movies
by Ruth Fowler

"Sorry, do you mind if I squeeze through?" I ask sheepishly.

"No problem, love," says the middle-aged bloke as he stands from his seat, plastic lager in hand.

I hurriedly snake around 5 or 6 people to get to my seat, meanwhile dropping popcorn as I manoeuvre like a kind of semiotic for finding my way out later. I sit down; put my ticket stub back in my wallet, in case I need to prove that I've paid again later. This has never actually happened by the way, but my neurosis won't let me do otherwise.

The adverts blare out Kevin Bacon selling EE contracts and I feel suitably depressed at what's happened to his career. If I were here with a friend I'd say, "Can you believe what's happened to him?"

I put my phone on silent and as I do I feel the brush of someone's arm on mine. A blonde woman has sat next to me; she's wearing heels and Hermes perfume. What the fuck is she doing here, she's not gay — although she could be a lipstick, I argue with myself as Bacon now becomes Chewbacca.

The drumroll starts and I get that tingly feeling that I always get when I'm at the cinema. I quickly start to make a mental note of where everything is: cinema stub in wallet, feet on floor, plastic cup by foot, about an inch away from toes, phone on lap on silent, arm on armrest but not too close to either neighbouring party. Even the fucking cinema has borders! And then, as if by some awful reminder not to have too much fun, his name is emblazoned across the screen. He is a reminder that misogyny is even at the lesbian film. The blonde woman mumbles, "Weinstein, no!" "I agree Hun," I want to say, "why is *Carol* produced by him?" I want to say, "Do you think he's raped her?" I want to say – but I don't, I just sit quietly as the film starts.

Oh fuck, why do I always do this? I'm so angry with myself, why do I think I can drink so much without needing a slash? My bladder has always been shit. "Sorry, can I squeeze through?" I say to Hermes. "Yep," she says. I weave through, and make big leaps up the steps in a kind of walking on the moon way as if it's going to distract everyone from the fact that I need a piss twenty minutes in.

I open the door and it sucks shut and bangs; my moonwalk was a pointless exercise. The space outside the cinema is reminiscent of a time before Bacon lost his career and I neurotically measured the distance in CM's from big toe to little toe. I bet I'm gonna miss the sex scene, I think to myself as I wee a bit like a horse, strong stream running into the toilet. I could just leave now and not go back in. It's actually the right thing to do, I think. I've actually really disturbed everyone by coming for this piss, yep; the admirable thing to do would be to leave now.

"Excuse me, sorry, can I squeeze through again?"

"No problem, love, you've just missed Carol getting touched up by a lezzer and I'm all hard" – and at that moment the whole fucking world stops. As I weave past the erect middle-aged bloke, I can't actually believe what's just been said. The blonde in heels clocked it and as I sit back down she whispers, "What.The.Fuck."

I run through all the possibilities of what's just happened: Agenda item number 1. Matters arising from my earlier exchange with him – seemed decent. Item number 2. Thinks he's funny – ACTION find out if he is. Item number 3. Is a total pervy homophobe? ACTION likely.

"Are you ok?" I whisper to blondey, who I think now is probably a lezzer. Why am I asking her if she's ok? I just got verbally assaulted and harassed. "Yeah he's a creep, are you ok?" That's nice of her to care back, I think to myself. Shit, is my phone still on aeroplane mode? "Yeah, but him, Kevin Bacon, and Weinstein have really ruined this film. Poor Carol," I say. She grimaces awkwardly like white people do when colonialism gets discussed. She turns back to the movie and I do too, making sure that my arm doesn't touch hers.

Blackthorn
by Kate Gallon

She is wrist deep in mud, fingers and palm chewed by the hole's mouth. The Earth swallows everything eventually. Her anger rises from her knees- bent in twelve Summers to no-one and nothing- for she is here, under the blackthorn. Again. She stabs her flint in to the dirt. Again, again. Sound pools in her throat.

Was there a time when she was not elbow-deep in muck? Before- there was mud of the river; dust of the rushes; shit of the babies - think no more of that, Matill. After- the tilling, the threshing, the midwifing to cattle. That Day- when they had thrown open the church to the roaming beasts, filling the mouths of the chiselled saints with cow shit; felling the sod nailed to his cock; dragging him in their braes up the hill- even That Day- the night of That Day- when she picked her way home on angels' wings, cleansed; long locks untied and lashing about her face the scent of bonfire. Even That Day her bare arms were crusted brown, her cheekbones stiff with salt, her nails charred black.

The taste of the air about her has changed and even with downcast eyes she knows that soon it will rain. Her flint cast aside, she leans in to the hole, pulling out rank clots and flinging them to her right, to her left. Every time she has been here, she has been doing this. She has done her duty by these, she knows. She knows where she is, where they are, at all times. Her body remembers them, her dreams too sometimes, but they never keep her from sleep. Matill thinks of Hab.

She will not say 'the problem of Hab' although she hears it said, feels it as a creeping shadow across her chest. Her son, ploughed in to her against the pig sty by Hudde- grunting and slobbering- the day he left, whilst she watched the clouds over his shoulder, drifted with them in to the tops of the oaks. It was always the way of it: Hudde the Warrior fucked her like this; Hudde the Farmer, slow and expert, disappeared up her cunt to be seen again only after the last of the warrior's scabs had been flicked to the floor. Hudde the Farmer, so far as she knew, was still up there.

The sty, and nine plump moons, and then Hab. He was nearing two years old That Day- not yet a man left behind by men, and hardly even a boy. He was round; a lump of shining clay that had not seen the potter's hand. Her son- yes- but one mouth amongst many. A seventh child, of those still living. Matill does not know when Hab became her daughter. In those early days- thrilling and dangerous and new- everyone was a 'sister', everyone a 'daughter'. She barely noticed that he wasn't until he was. And now, perceptible only when still- sleeping perhaps, back-lit by the dying hearth- her daughter was growing a beard.

The rain slaps the ground and the worms answer. All activity is here; delighted, they writhe. Her bundle to her chest; thinks of bed, of woman, of ways she will be kept warm. Later, later; but first... it is the setting down that is the worst of it. She sees the barley fields below, empty stalks now; imagines them back in to being. Conjures from her goosebumps the shudder of sun on the back of her neck. How short the walk from his beginning to his ending. How short hers will also be. Always work; more work than before, to be sure, but better work; better work. Always work- and Hab pushing her way in from the corners of Matill's mind; Hab, with her jaw stretching and her cheeks filling, pushing her way in to the minds of the other women. And behind Hab, Hudde. And behind Hudde, all of the gone husbands, all of the gone sons; all of the Holy fucking Our Fathers that they had set to blaze That Day up on the heather. She had not thought of husband in many, many moons until Hab's shape-shifting had begun; Hudde's tools, his clothes, by now entirely infused with the scent and toil of Matill herself. Of the farm, he would only recognise the contoured face of the land, such are the changes she has wrought upon crops and animals. In her element, Matill casts her seeds down in to the depths and the Earth vomits up bounty after glorious bounty. She had planted the barley field down there with Hab just as Hudde's face had begun sprouting upon that delicate neck stalk. That had been the start of it; 'quod seminas ita metes'. She shakes her head and the quote is sent hurtling out of her ears, dispelled by the wind to land on the lap of some other fucker; thinks: some magic at work in it, though- She did sow Hudde, and Hudde she did reap. Some semblance of him. For as the barley had pushed up shoots, so he had again taken root. She churned upon him as she formed her butter. She hauled upon him as she raised her bucket. And then, in the barley field, arse aloft, glistening by efforts of the sun and her weeding combined, flushed in all her cheeks and wanting filling, she saw Hudde turn the corner up by the hazel trees. Heart-stopping. The barley playing tricks on her, she knew, by the time this Hudde was close by. Back to her senses in mind, if not in body, she had him anyway; coaxed him off the path with some bullshit about needing a stone moving and would Sire be ever so inconvenienced. The joke of it; her biceps making his seem pale and brittle. A tanner, she thought, by the reek of him. Alone afterwards- cocooned in her flattened patch of stalks and his lingering stench of fermented cow piss- she caught a glimpse of the blackthorn; thought nothing of it.

The bundle is in the ground now. To the tanner, a son; to the worms, a feast. Matill pares with her front teeth one of the two apples that she has brought with her to lay; the first thing she has wanted to eat all day. Burials are for the living. Fruits are for the living too, but the oldest ways are the hardest to vanquish and she gently places the remaining apple at the feet of baby, meat of her meat. Frozen to her marrow, she raises herself up to standing and, smashing her teeth through pip and core, heaves the first earth back in to the grave with her clogge.

She wants, is the truth of it. This is what the tanner, perversely, has taught her. She has writhed with some number of the women across the telescoping years; left, for a time, her grounded, Earth-fast nature, and been the thunder, streaking sharp. She wants to build altars to gods she no longer believes in, to bind and be bound, to hunt and quest and build; to keep someone. Her lovers will not be kept. Undisturbed, they accept her reflection for a moment but they hold nothing of her, and cannot be held. They have burned Christ; that is burning enough for their waters. They have had their husbands and do not want another. Matill stamps a frantic rhythm upon the mound as the driving rain percusses all about her. She wants a world that will fit inside the circle of her arms. She wants.

Powering down the hill, a torrent of pure white energy, Matill knows what she must do and is resolved- "They go", she shouts to the trees, the moss, the river. They fucking go, and so will fucking she- to a place where a woman may take a wife and a girl may have a prick. She wades towards her hut, through her corrugated fields, storms her outbuildings, collecting tools, pots, skins, almost at random. She is the wind, is the sky, is the fire- the hut, an outline of a door, comes in to view- is the fire, is the thunder, but first- she must cook; then she must clean; then she must, then she must… then she must…

Gofod

gan Kate Gallon

Rwy'n cerdded drwy'r tŷ

pob drws yn agor i le sydd newydd wagio.

Tegell poeth
Peiriant golchi ar delicate
Llinellau sialc o fwg yn codi o cannwyll fach

Rwyt ti mewn ystafell arall

neu

rwyt ti'n cerdded.

Rwyt ti'n cerdded dros y bryn.
Rwyt ti'n cerdded ar draws y dibyn.
Rwyt ti'n cerdded Aisle 14 eto oherwydd weithiau nid yw pethau lle

                                            gadewaist

                    nhw

Mae octopws uwchben yn torri ei gysgod corduroi ar draws
dy gyflwr meddwl
nofio i ddram curiad dy galon
sugnwyr yn sgimio dy foch
tentaclau ym mhob man

Growing
by Kate Gallon

      When I look back   to the time when we meant
nothing to each other
it will be today that I'm   thinking of

     Tomorrow and tomorrow and tomorrow and
tomorrow and tomorrow and tomorrow and tomorrow and
tomorrow and tomorrow she and I will grow you

      Not in any cavity   between our hips

                      You will begin between our
ears

                      between our teeth

                      falling off the tip of
                              our
                        tongues

but tomorrow
today we mean nothing to each other

You will compete for space with frontal lobe parietal lobe
ventral visual pathways stems and cerebrum   You will
emerge from parts of our bodies that we never truly knew
existed
fathered by neurogenesis

Today I am walking and sitting and sipping and standing
Today maybe you too? How old are you?

it will be today that I'm
              thinking of   when I look back

What will you be
    thinking of   when you look back

                              when we look back together

Gwerful Mechain's Genitals
by Kate Gallon

Let songs to the quim circulate
without fail to gain reward
Gwerful Mechain

How Mechains's Churchmen

    Poets

   Her Wizards, even

  turn from

      it

How even as they want it

    touch it

      fuck it with a spoon

    cannot, do not give it voice

How the oral smock is unlifted

How dark

How invisible

How bright Saints' tongues stay still

How quaint they are

How hypocritical

How impoverished

How times change

How Churchmen

    Journalists

        Strangers in clubs

            in bars

            in fucking Tesco

Unzip my jeans with their teeth

    their social media

    their broken bottles

Debate mine

    in public

        without ceasing

Home
by Kate Gallon

this is home- each season brings its own variety of roadkill a cat not mine drags it to the door the drive is steep steep

this is home- which category best describes your sexual orientation heterosexual gay lesbian transgender

this is home- tiny underpants lost are found hibernating fiercely tight tight in the corners of pillowcases

this is home- katy perry kisses a girl whilst thinking about her boyfriend I guess in the winter Vaseline is involved or similar

this is home- another funeral procession face-off on a single track road it is part of the ritual ritual they take it in turns to back down I notice

this is home- the hedgehog begins at the tail the slow worm is conscious throughout throughout is this the same as television or worse

the hedgehog begins at the tail the slow worm is conscious throughout throughout is this the same as television or worse - this is not home

another funeral procession face-off on a single track road it is part of the ritual ritual they take it in turns to back down I notice - this is not home

katy perry kisses a girl whilst thinking about her boyfriend I guess in the winter Vaseline is involved or similar
- this is not home

tiny underpants lost are found hibernating fiercely tight tight in the corners of pillowcases- this is not home

which category best describes your sexual orientation
heterosexual gay lesbian transgender- this is not home

each season brings its own variety of roadkill a cat not mine
drags it to the door the drive is steep steep- this is not home

Blonde or Brunette?
by Annabelle May Hampton

Suspended in time
Our eyes lock
Hate? Indifference? Love?
Who knows?

Your mask resumes its composure
I gaze straight ahead
Continue my journey
Thinking about your roots
And how black they have become

Old roses
Hidden from the sun
Petals falling one by one
Scented, black
But always dead

Silken dreams
Hate slipping
Blue eyes and blonde hair
Icy blasts
Love dripping
Nothing can save your soul
From pity.

Blonde or Brunette
by Annabelle May Hampton

The infatuation came fast and died hard
Blue eyes and blonde hair
Nothing can save the blackened roots
For pity's sake you must beware

Cold dawn and clear sight
Blue eyes and blonde hair
The mask slips out of control
No more goodbyes
Just empty gestures
Cardboard smiles

Coincidence
by Annabelle May Hampton

A Midlands town, back alleyway, foggy, late evening, yellow neon light. A Russian built 650cc motorcycle, horizontally opposed engine, military style sidecar. A prehistoric beast waiting for its keeper.

Make-up, stockings, dress etc. The helmeted figure throws the holdall into the sidecar.

No-one will suspect, unlikely trip, unlikely transport, machismo preserved. Tickle the carbs, smell the petrol, six dead kicks, ignition on. A quick, sharp kick, the machine fires. Rev the throttle, leave it to tick over, three to four times at least. Depress clutch, boot it into first; the beast burbles gently as it edges towards the main road.

The Triumph must have been doing 70, it skids, narrowly missing the sidecar, a loose bungee and there lying in the road a holdall. The rider manages to stop and looks back. Leaving the bike ticking over he puts it on the sidestand and runs quickly back to retrieve the holdall. A cursory nod to the fellow biker, the cargo bungeed back on, he speeds off into the night. The sidecar rider, about to continue, something catches his attention. In the gutter a size 9 patent stiletto … …

Identity
by Annabelle May Hampton

The structure of the end is complicated, he said.

The problem is the process of transition, he said.

The end is near, she said.

Life But Not As I Know It
by Annabelle May Hampton

I love you, hate you, think that you are beautiful
Ugly want to fuck you leave you
Think you are blonde brunette want to
Touch, untouchable
You made sure I would never feel your
Leg against mine again but it's still there
Like an amputated limb.

My First Dress
by Annabelle May Hampton

Age 7, a small garden in a small town. The Black Country, grimy, industrial and mean spirited. Summer 1961.

Raindrops the size of small marbles churn up the hard packed earth that forms most of the "garden". Lightning strikes, everything changes. Excited, scared and alone I run towards the rotting fence at the back. Looking down the steep embankment clouds of smoke erupt from a passing steam train. It deafens, threatens and is relentless. The smoke conspires with the storm to turn the whole scene black, an impenetrable mass.

For a moment I lose my sense of place and I stamp my small feet on the sodden ground, partly to reassure myself that the ground is still beneath me but more in a frenzy of ecstasy; change is possible, things don't have to stay the same. The garden lights up again, thunder follows. Slowly the downpour ceases, the deluge has washed everything clean. The flowers that decorated the fence are a brilliant white. I always thought they were grey…..

"STEEE-VEN", … My mom shouts from the back door. This time real fear takes hold, nowhere to run.

The girls from next door have gone inside, the door shut, no hiding place. The gate in the yard bangs open, footsteps up the path, past the privet hedge that formed the perfect screen. My mom looms into sight.

Trembling and very much alone, in a wet pink satin dress with big puffed sleeves and an enormous bow, resplendent in dainty silver shoes, I cannot move. I am frightened but another emotion is also present, an overwhelming sense of relief. The secret was out.

My mom's face. Disappointment, confusion, anger, bewilderment: "WOT THE BLUDDY ELL YOW DRESSED IN, DUN YOW KNOW YOW'RE A BOY NOT A WENCH?"

I didn't really hear the words and was led, not unkindly back to my house. We crossed the back yard.

"WOTCH ME FROCK, ME MAM'LL KILL ME IF IT GETS RIPPED", the girl from next door shouts through her window. My Mom replies "DUNNA FRET DEAR IT'LL BE WASHED AND RETURNED TOMORRA". She looks at me then mutters "BUT HE WUNNA".

Then, looking directly into my eyes she says, "YOW THINK I DUN KNOW DON'T YOW. I DUNNA WURRY BUT AS FER YOW DAD … YOW GORRA UNNERSTAND, YOW'RE A BOY, IT'S GORRA STOP".

The back door, Dad fills it, my twin brother peeps out from behind his legs, "TOLD YOW IT'UD GET YOW INTA TRUBBLE" he smirks. My dad says nothing, just stares, turns and walks inside. His policy was simple, removal from risk. I never saw the girls from next door again. He sent me to play with an older boy a few doors away to do 'Boy things', football and the like.

Anyway, He turned out to be gay, and dressed me up in his mom's clothes, but that's another story …….

This Is Your Vagina (My Latest Painting)
by Annabelle May Hampton

This is your vagina
It is also a :-
Self portrait
The spirit of my dead twin
The storm before the calm
My relationship with my son
But in the end
This is how I perceived and understood
A landscape
Thawed by my gaze
Scrutinised by the mind's eye
Dissected by analysis
Crucified by obsession
A collection of marks
Meaning peculiar to self
Not forgetting :-
White spirit
Linseed oil
A process of manufactured
Manipulated paint.

Towards An End
by Annabelle May Hampton

The year moves relentlessly
Towards its final display
I continue to make marks
Unsure of the result
The canvas groans
I know the direction
Skeletal fingers beckon
And seem to herald a journey
A portent of change
An examination of self.
The sky forces my eye upwards
The window winks at me
And I am again reminded
That this may be destiny's jest.

Show and Tell
by Nic Herriot

'Hang on a mo. That's so out of order.'

I pull Joanne's sleeve, stopping her advance on the boiled fruit cakes.

A staple of every show, it's one of the toughest to crack - and in my opinion a waste of a bloody good fruit cake. At the end of a hot afternoon it's hard to distinguish between a burnt raisin and a house fly or three.

Taking a short cut via the Dahlias I whisk her to the craft sections. The Dahlias are a hotly contested section, not to mention each flower-head is close to 8 inches in diameter, so my impassioned move past twenty three vases top heavy with vast blooms is quite tricky, but I'm on a mission.

'Look at that!'

'Shush, you're being too loud, - again.'

'I want to be loud, this is an outrage.' I deliver my dissatisfaction in a stage whisper. 'How do you lodge a complaint? This is blatant cheating.'

I wave the supposedly hand-crafted item in the air. It's a colourfully constructed article with thin scraps of plastic woven into the twists of the wire frame to make a small chicken that, admittedly, sits well on the table. My Granny would mutter 'dust collector' under her breath if she saw it. Sadly, Joanne is the only one paying me any attention.

The vicar squeezes past on his way to the tea stall. You get a Welsh cake or bara brith with your choice of beverage, for only a £1. His diet isn't going too well and I'm squashed into

the table edge. A couple of women are peering at the preserves on the table opposite - tutting. Not a good sign. Put your strawberry jam in a recycled jar with a hint of its previous occupant and you risk the wrath of the judges, the scorn of every villager over the age of 50, and the possibility of never showing your face again.
It's one of the many gender free classes which is currently being ruled in the county by a man in his 70's.

My English mother-in-law sweeps up the certificates at her village show, so, when she found herself visiting us one year in show season, she brought some of her award-winning preserves. The jars didn't get opened; or if they were, the judges didn't bother to taste. I innocently enquired as to their seemingly not being assessed and the errors were explained. One jar top had the fruit printed on the rim… it being an ex-supermarket jam jar, this is just not done, and the other… it had a grease-proof circle protecting the contents. The judge simply does not have the time to remove the paper from every jar. Maybe it's all in a name, Mum-in-law's Show being called "The Meadow Lark", I mean, how cuddly does that sound? I bet everyone gets to win a prize.

Enough of that, back to today's travesty.

'How do you know it's not homemade? It's in the locals only section - she could be good with creating things out of recycled items.'

 With the conviction of a Victorian hanging judge, as by now I feel the competitor should be… hung… not judged, I turn the offending article over and show Joanne the tiny silver 'made in china' label on the leg and proclaim that you can buy these for a fiver a time in any gift shop.

'Maybe she thought the section was "craft *bought* for under £5".

Joanne withers under my stare. The defence might've been sound if this was any other section. Over the years new comers do misunderstand the rules. On one occasion someone entered four hens eggs; the unstated rule being eggs from your own hens… these had the British Lion symbol stamped on each of them. Then there was the year of the apples, four lovely gala apples, all complete with their certified organic stickers!

'How do I launch an inquiry?' I'm still cross that no one is paying me any attention.

'Find a steward, someone with a rosette.' Joanne is sidling away back to the cakes. I find a rosetted person.

'Excuse me.' I try to engage with her, but she is engrossed in "Remembering the Fallen. 1914-1918. An all foliage and fruit exhibit. 48cm by 48cm," It's an emotional trestle table of flora dedicated to the Great War.

I move to her other side in an attempt to cut off her chance to observe "Pink Blush, a petit exhibit 25cm by 25cm." In doing so I spot Joanne being very attentive to the butterfly cakes, special category for children.

'I think someone has cheated, in the craft section…'

She edges towards the Blushes, I hold my ground. '…in the craft section, it's a ringer…' Blank look. 'It's a bought in chicken, not home-made.'

She still looks disinterested. I check out her chest, yep, the rosette is still there.

'Look, I want to show you.' I point over to the offending article, intercepting her approach to Miniature Garden, 20cm x 20cm, height not to exceed 10cm another class popular with adults and children alike and involving lots of canny tricks with mirrors and broccoli florets.
She finally follows my arm and peers over to the 'Confined to Residents of…' craft table. She reads the red certificate next to the chicken. That's why I'm mildly irritated. The woman got a First!!

'That's Gwendoline Hughes, she is a member of the Show Committee, she wouldn't cheat, she would've made it herself.'

End of discussion as the steward returns to the flower arrangements. I am defeated but still indignant that justice was not served. The raffle is drawing the crowd back in, and I've had to detour my disheartened way via Succulents in Pots to Joanne at the rear of the hall.

'What did you expect?' No sympathy from my beloved. 'Anyway, you've not gone by the rules either.' She smugly points to small paragraph on the inside front cover of the program.

'"Any protest has to be made in writing, accompanied by a fee of 50p." Harassing a steward does not an enquiry make.'

'But you said, you told me…'

Even this complaint wasn't being heard as I'm bundled out of the building - just as I hear my ticket being called.

'Hey, that's mine, they're calling my number. This could be your last chance to have that dusty 'Scents of Christmas' candle, or the shell encrusted Chianti bottle-lamp…'

'This is *your* last chance to get out of here alive; I have to face this lot at the school gates on Monday.' I finally concede defeat with a grin, 'Yes Miss, I love it when you go all head teacher on me.'

Pretending to Protest
by Maj Ikle

1983 starts slow I find myself singing along to Duran Duran's 'Hungry like the Wolf' and after a horrid xmas with my divorced parents at each other's throats I am even more determined to find a new girlfriend. I've had enough of the rad fem scene, with its expanding rules and dwindling membership. The idea that anything less than simultaneous orgasm is abusive, is doing my head in.

Instead I was becoming increasingly intrigued by the hand-illustrated DIY leaflets being sent out to women's groups by Greenham Common women's peace camp. For hours I pore over their funny and carefully handwritten stories about living exclusively around other women passionate about stopping war and nuclear weapons. All year round in rain, sun, sleet or snow, women get arrested, sent to prison and then go immediately back to the base to do it all over again, I'm inspired.

I decide I have to go and see this utopia for myself. I put up posters inviting women to a 'hands around the base' demo and because I'm the women's officer am able to wrangle the student union minibus.

Early on that cold March morning, breath smoking from our nostrils like horses we loaded up with tents and the rest of our stuff. In my enthusiasm however, it seemed I had promised more seats than were actually in the bus. With much huffing and puffing the seps have to squeeze up tight to the 'straight' women in the group muttering darkly like bickering owls anytime anyone mentioned a male child let alone a boyfriend gave the journey a tense vibe.

That was until on the M4 to Newbury we caught sight of the actual sign to RAF Greenham Common where someone, had sprayed a triple women's symbol all over the massive motorway sign and the whole bus erupted into shrieks of delight.

From then an increasing number of peace and women's symbols appear on the road signs until the main entrance comes into view. Women are everywhere. From toothless babies to wrinkled crones they spill out of cars, sit picnicking on the grass, or gather in groups laughing and hugging each other like family. Some thread ribbons through the fence to make pictures of doves and peace symbols, others paint the road with splashy proclamations 'here to stay til the missiles go away'. The fun and optimism of the place is a festival as much as a protest.

I'd had to sign a piece of paper to say I accepted responsibility to personally pay for any damage to the minibus so I'm fussy about where we leave it. Most of the gates have been a complete wreck of mud until we arrive at one where the layout seems less chaotic 'Welcome to Orange Gate,' is scrawled in drippy paint on the road. Each of the nine gates being named after a colour of the rainbow. As I haul my pack I notice I am shivery with adrenal excitement from this unfamiliar feeling of being in the company of thousands of people all women.

Once we are all out of the bus it's obvious that we aren't planning to make an 'East London Polytechnic camp' together so I strike out alone determined to keep to my plan of making new friends. I am brought up short though staring through the chain link fence for a moment. I can see actual American nuclear missile tips in the distance real and intransigent.

Like freshly sharpened pencils, red rings painted onto sleek white, they are ready for business. The missiles line up efficiently in their silos while the women's peace camp sprawls the other side of the fence. New circles of tents blooming colours onto the empty scrubland. Permanently erect, ready at four minutes notice to commence a war of mutually assured destruction for the whole world. It's literally MAD.

Because of them though, here are we, women celebrating this International Women's Day theme of peace. Us mere women, only good for soft jobs unless we pretend to be men like Thatcher and cosy up to arms dealers have no political power. But, like an army of ants, the sheer weight of our numbers and determination are drawing the eyes of the world onto Greenham Common Airbase and how Britain is being used as America's boxing glove.

Women who live here sleep under sheets of grubby clear plastic tarpaulin thrown over a pegged down tree. This makes no sense to me so I sit down at a smoky firepit to ask why they don't just camp in proper tents. I'm told in a weary voice that daily evictions mean that they have no camping equipment left at all. Almost everyday warrants issued by the local courts are enforced by bailiffs and a team of bin men come to commandeer and destroy everything they can find belonging to the women, which they do with apparent relish.

Because of this constant tearing down women have learned to live with only the amount of stuff that can be held in their arms during an eviction hence the clear plastic and sleeping bags. This has been their lives for nearly ten years already. I stare at the muddy puddles inside the so-called 'benders.' They must be more robust or built differently to me I tell myself, these women are able to withstand cold and misery better than I could. I try to pin this theory onto the older women who live there but I have to have a very big spliff to make it stick.

I continue my journey towards the communal fire nearest the gate, where a women drinks tea oblivious to the fact that her suckling baby has fallen off asleep. There is happy singing everywhere and great cackling gutsy laughter coming from all directions, women embrace with one another deeply, it is obvious they enjoy the feeling of their bodies connecting together in friendship or sexual love.

Suddenly everywhere I look women seem to be kissing and touching one another. Is it me or has a sexual shiver spread through even the women I would have had down as straight. The air itself seems to be a wild aphrodisiac. Women who were talking about campaigning themselves into prison one minute ago, now open their mouths to pleasure one another.

I study the fire. Blackened kettles displaying melted barely graspable plastic handles threatening to topple at the smallest shift of a log. Around the fire circle is a blast site, a muddy ring beyond which, on the only patch of grass left, someone has made fake shelves out of milk crates. There is a melted washing up bowl and drainer filled with mugs, everything is filthy on the outside but reasonably clean where it counts sort of functionally post-apocalyptic.

Thirsty, I wonder when someone who know the ropes will offer me tea. It seems only fair after how far we've come to support them but no one makes me anything even when they make some for other women around the fire and all of them seem completely fussy about what kind of tea they want and what kind of special milk they need. Finally I get offered a filthy mug of something that someone else didn't want.

Wondering what other kind of milk there is, I watch two women drag a ludicrously heavy plastic container of water two hundred yards from a standpipe set by the gate. Despite an old ladies shopping trolley that seems almost completely submerged beneath the mud, they keep pulling and pushing until they arrive at the pretend kitchen area and park the water on an upturned log.

I sip, not sure if it is coffee or tea but aware now how grateful I am to have a wet warm drink. Periodically the burning wood shifts, causing the contents of the kettle to spill out and douse the flames. I watch this scene happen twice more before finally, sufficient steam is blasted from the blackened spout for the water to be deemed 'properly boiling'.

If it is this hard to make tea, I realise, I'm not going to be moving in and joining the permanent protest community. My romantic utopian vision of a lesbian paradise was, all hot chocolate and sex in tents, not this grim determination needed to make even one cup of tea.

Meanwhile everyone around me is snogging or fondling with fervent desire. I look around to see how to extricate myself. From out of an old brown kitchen tent that had seen many healthier days, a woman calls for 'volunteers to chop veg?' Up shoots my 'eager to escape' hand. After a sort of snort, she motions towards a sack of carrots and I gush "happy to help."

I sit staring at a filthy carrot, hoping someone will join me in this going-to-take-all-day job. Then photos are being taken of me beside the mountain of carrots and women have begun to ask questions about the location of the shit-pits and what time lunch will be ready. At first, I motion towards the real 'Greenham women' inside but after realising this is winding them up I just relay the instructions I've heard instead and enjoy the raw admiration I see in the photographers eyes. From inside the tent though I can also hear anxious raised voices about how many of the visitors were going to "stay here with us?"

Finally, after what feels like 3 hours, I am relieved of carrot peeling duties and my carrots are added to the stew. I am encouraged by the appreciative cooks to jump to the front of the enormous queue but once this is done I become a mere weekender all over again. I keep my head down in case anyone has noticed my sudden demotion.

The next day is Sunday and the time of the big action for which we had all come. Women have dressed up and many of them have peace symbols painted on their faces and bright hedge flowers in their hair. Some hold up mirrors to reflect to the soldiers what they look like to us and try to entreat them to act peacefully, they don't engage. There are many more of us than them. Women sing easy to learn chants and rounds about peace and no more war.

After about an hour, women start sitting down on the ground facing the eight-foot high gate singing; "all we are saying; is give peace a chance." It is only four years since John Lennon was killed. A spine quivering spirit of peace fills the air, like a choir of thrushes, our high sweet voices rise as American soldiers begin to line up inside the fence to face down our 'terrorist threat'.

I suddenly feel totally part of what is going on, I'm not sure if it is the quality of the singing that has given me a sort of ecstatic connection but I'm sure I can feel the embryonic buds of my activist bones solidify. Something more important than getting women to fancy me is calling now, stopping the destruction of this beautiful planet.

For a moment, we are all held in a glorious equilibrium. Us, choiring peace solutions. Them, our dark male opposites, preparing to protect their weapons of mass destruction. Then the British police on our side of the fence suddenly start the process of dragging women away from the gate to make way for the missiles coming out, I watch horrified as they scrape them a long way on the road as if we were bags of rubbish.

Someone whispers to me how I will be heavier if I 'go limp,' so I pass it on as a whisper to the women sitting next to me. Linking arms, we nod in a promise to one another that we will to stay put whatever happens.

I watch white knuckled policeman's hands try to haul up the women sitting alongside me. It is hard to think limp when the anxiety adrenaline kicks in about where and how those hands will grab you. They work in teams of four or five as the floppy bodies need to be held in many places but we are easily dropped. The indignity of having disrespectful hands pulling at my droopy body doesn't put me off. For once in my life I am more afraid of the effect of those missiles on my whole world if I do nothing.

It is at that very moment with the pleas for peace ringing the air that one of the seps bends over to remind me that I have to drive the minibus. If I get arrested they will be left stranded.

Two-Thousand-Eighteen
by Maj Ikle

A dandelion
dawn dew settles in to sculpt
elderly afros

as spring pillions us
into summer like bees
on motorbikes

til a warm Welsh haze
contents naked dykes who bask
in birdsong freedom.

Vagitus
by Maj Ikle

Alice is constantly crying
it's unfeasibly easy how hurt
Alice feelings can be
if it's not late at night till quarter past three
I find her sobbing every mealtime
into soup, lemon drizzle cake or morning tea.

I say Alice
'aren't you ashamed
of being so thoroughly wet'
but the more I ask the louder Alice protests get
'can't you see my needs' she says
between snivelling snotted sniffs
'aren't even nearly (let alone really) being met?

I turn away from her displays
for fear she
will lure me into defensive ways
instead I eat like a pig
mouth open as I munch
hoping to drown her lament
in flagrant mastication.

I even offer to leave her to find someone
who can mend her broken heart and mind
that is when Alice reaches for the skies of her sighs
bursts into a squall of
such biblical blubbering that
the pitch of her howls
would open wounds in you

so deep that to mend them
would take surgical glue.

Baby I say
Tell me what task I can perform
To sop up this sea for both you and me
To end what it is that offends or ails you
Then Alice replies with more red
than is good in her eyes
she stares swollen cheeked
from her salt soaked enterprise
'tell me you love me...no matter what'
and because
it is true...I do

Honour
by Mair Jones

She deserved honour.
Which foolish men didn't give.
For her pretty face
Smooth, silken body and golden hair.

These were taken away.
Punished for the crimes of men.
Replaced with hard
Ugliness.

Rough hands,
green eyes,
green hair,
hissing.

She turns you to stone.
She keeps you away;
the foolish men
kept at bay.

Panicked eyes
in their stone prisons.

Loneliness. Except
for her pet snakes,
from her smooth scalp.
They bite you away.

Hide her face
which hurts everyone.
Keep her away
her stone heart

and deadly eyes,

Hissing hair,
covers her face,
she screams,
they hiss.

God didn't save her,
but she used her punishment,
to punish the crimes of men.
And turn herself to stone.

- Medusa

Balchder a Bysedd
gan Mair Jones

Mae pethau *eraill* yn gweithio'n iawn hefyd.
Pethau rwyt ti'n defnyddio i gyrraedd tu fewn i fi,
i ddod ag ysgrydau trwy fy nghorff i gyd.

Ond dy dwylo yw fy hoff offeryn rwyt ti'n ei ddefnyddio.

Dwylo meddal dros ystumau fy ngorff i gyd,
yn cyffwrdd â fi ymhobman.
Dy fysedd tu fewn i fi, yn araf ac yn slic,
yn teimlo pob rhan ohona i...
Mae dy gyffwrdd yn fanwl, yn ofalus, yn berffaith.

Ti'n berffaith.

Fel mae ein cyrff gyda'i gilydd
fel mynyddoedd -
jyst yn ffitio
yn hollol naturiol,
yn berffaith.

Dy anadal di fel hanfod dy fywyd,
dy enaid yn fy erbyn i,
yn amgylchynu fi, yn dal arna i –
fel dy freichiau o fy amgylch nawr
wrth i ni gorwedd nôl i lawr,
yn gyflawn yn ein gilydd.

Perffaith.

Ode To All That Is Woman
by Mair Jones

A response to 'Cywydd Y Cedor' by Gwerful Mechain (1460-1502), translated as 'The Female Genitals' by Dafydd Johnston.[1.]

'Sidan ydiw.' *(It is silk.)*

Every drunken fool
gives fruitless praise
to her body
- soft breasts,
long blonde hair,
and the <u>shape</u> of her.

'Foelder dwyfron feddaldwf.' *(Smoothness of soft breasts.)*

Praising the corporeal,
her physical self,
whiteness of her skin
- skin deep praise
of her body,
her <u>purity</u>.

'Boorish vanity without ceasing.'

Mae hi'n sidan. *(She is silk.)*
'He pays homage to God's greatness.'
Not only neglecting the warm quim,
or womanhood in all shapes -
cunt or not, *she*
is full of love.

She is softness, kindness in her soul;
beauty in her eyes, her gaze on you;
on her tongue, her sharp words;
inspiration comes from her;
her difference, attracting.
'She a boundless body of strength.'

The fools, drunks, poets,
can keep their weak, superficial praises,
while I, we, see all there is
to praise in woman - women
- from tender fatness,
to lovely bush.

Duw'n borth iddi.

1. Gwyn Griffiths, Meic Stephens eds. *The Old Red Tongue: An Anthology of Welsh Literature from the 6th to the Early 21st Century*, London, 2017, pp. 301-302.

Pulse
by Matthew Woolfall Jones

We stand together in the bay:
Heads bowed.
Chests tight.
Hearts pounding.
The dragon flies overhead on its multi-coloured canvas,
quiet falls.
Our silence is a guard:
Against the pain.
Against unnecessity.
Against hate.

This rank crime was not a passionate cause.

Passion is getting yourself out into the city.
It's getting yourself onto that dancefloor.
It's love and laughter and the pulse of the one you hold.

Our passion is communal –
A jigsaw of souls, our chests linked and pulsating,
Synced with Christopher and Juan, they've just started dating;
With Xavier, a professional dancer, a father of one;
And Brenda, just beaten cancer, out with her gay son.

This pulsing city,
this pulsing beat,
It is our pulse and it drums,
It rings loud and clear
Every day.
Every day.
Every day.

But not today
Today it has skipped

There's a faded stamp on my hand.
Saturday's remnant.
My pass to my safe place.
My entry to Pulse nightclub, Cardiff.
But as our Pulse boomed and banged and laughter roared
Another Pulse, in another city was paused.

And so we stand here
We are united
Entwined and entangled in love and grief
As their names are reeled off:

Stanley, Shane, Oscar, Rodolfo,
Alejandro, Martin, Darryl, Antonio,
Luis, Cory, Franky, Tevin,
Jonathan, Angel, Christopher and Juan,
Deonka, Mercedez, Peter, Paul,
Juan, Frank, Miguel, Joel,
Anthony, Jason, Luis, Eddie, Javier,
Kimberly, Christopher, Simon, Xavier,
Jean, Jerald, Eric, Geraldo,
Edward, Enrique, Luis, Gilberto,
Jean, Juan, Akyra, Amanda,
Luis, Leroy, Yilmary and Brenda.

I look at Robin and he looks at me,
and we know, this could have been us.

Mystery shopper
by Emma Lloyd

"It's an ACTUAL bowl!" Sam shrieks, as she fishes out a tiny parasol and slurps the maraschino cherry it's harpooning. The cocktail is a lurid shade of blue never found in nature, and it smells like that value-range squash that's allegedly generic 'fruit' flavour. It's semi-opaque and the slices of orange could almost be mistaken for goldfish if you squint hard enough.

"Not bad for six quid, though," I say, but Sam's busy sucking up her share, mouth pursed and cheeks concave. She replies with a wriggle of her eyebrows (which arch in a painstakingly perfect manner, I notice), and Kim Wilde's singing about Cambodia on the oldies channel on the telly above the fruit machine.

I lean towards the goldfish bowl to join Sam in hoovering up the Blue Meanie, and take a massive sip that unfortunately also includes a stray orange pip. Sam leaps up, reaches round my back and starts thumping, hard. Between coughs and wheezes I decide that if I die, here and now, it will be with a smile on my face and Sam's hands on my body - albeit intermittently.

Something shifts inside me, then shoots out of my mouth. I'm flailing around for a paper napkin to wipe my streaming eyes, and Sam looks shaken - concerned, even.

She likes me. I can tell.

The family on the next table are typically - Britishly - polite and thorough when it comes to hunting down the errant pip. The grandfather extracts it from a tiny tub of tartare sauce, and Sam giggles, "Good shot!" I'm using the now-soggy napkin to mop up my spray of saliva - which let's face, is kind of inevitable if someone's just nearly choked to death - but it's a surprise to see how far it's flown. The Nana brushes away my efforts, then refocuses on her fish and chips, ignoring my apologies.

We nearly crack heads as we bend towards our straws. We've nearly finished it already, and my cheeks are starting to burn. From this angle I can see straight down Sam's top, and my cheeks burn even more. Looking away - because staring is not an appropriate option just yet - I can see that Mr Fish and Chips family has also clocked the view of Sam's Hello Kitty bra and a tattoo that neither of us are close enough to read.

"You're giving Grandad an eyeful," I hiss.

"An EIFFEL?" she shouts. Frankie Goes to Hollywood are welcoming us to the PleasureDome, and all those *HOO! HA!*s are starting to overstimulate me. "Eiffel like the TOWER? What *are* you on about?"

"No!" I pantomime horror, pointing to my eyes. "An EYE FULL, of your-" and of course the song ends at this precise moment - "TITS!"

Mr Fish and Chips looks apoplectic, and the Nana's perm visibly stiffens as she pulls a cat's-bum face. Sam's laughing so hard that a sizeable spray of Blue Meanie erupts from her nostrils, all over the beer mats and my shirt. On the table next to us, anoraks are being zipped as Nana stashes some emergency ketchup in her handbag. I'm sure I hear her mutter something about the pub having *gone downhill since last summer* as they leave.

We're drunk: but then a jug of Mango Martini and a pitcher of Planter's Punch will do that to you, especially when chased with a goldfish bowl of fruit-flavoured, industrial grade meths.

"So you get all this for free?" asks Sam. "How does that work?"

"I signed up for this mystery shopping job online," I explain. "It's mostly quite dull stuff, but occasionally I get a 'Food and Drink' assignment. Like tonight, we're technically sampling the new cocktail menu and then I do a questionnaire scoring everything from flavour to ambience. I send a photo of my receipt - up to a certain amount - and they reimburse me by Paypal."

"That's so cool," says Sam, and I want to believe her. It's not quite The Ivy on an expenses account, but I like being able to treat her without hammering my overdraft. It certainly beats chips in the rain by the pier. Sam's running her finger down the lengthy cocktail menu.

"What do you fancy next?" she says.

I want to say Sex on the Beach, for hilarity's sake, but the fish and chip people are long gone and there's no-one else close enough to outrage, and maybe it would sound like I was flirting like an amateur (which, if I'm honest, is what my flirting always sounds like). I don't want Sam to think I'm like those leery guys by the fruit machine, even though they're mostly wearing those tan leather jackets beloved of CID and divorced blokes on the pull, and I'm wearing my black vintage bowling shirt which - thankfully - hasn't stained where Sam's drink splattered me although it does smell a bit noxious now.

I take the menu off her and scan it for something high in alcohol and low on innuendo.

"Let's try the Zombie," I say. Two types of fruit juice and three types of rum: what could possibly go wrong? The oldies music channel has reached 1989 when I reach the bar. It was a weird year for music: Soul II Soul kept on moving while Hue and Cry were looking for Linda, and Jive Bunny and the Mastermixers did terrible, unspeakable things.

The Zombie is a murky, inevitable green, and comes in a jug. They've run out of fruit which is probably a good thing from a Health & Safety point of view. Sam rolls her eyes as I skirt round the fruit machine guys with their wandering glances and #lolz and #bantz.

"Well, this is nice," she smiles, and in the space of a nanosecond I notice how the tips of her hair are the same shade of dirty turquoise as her eyes, and there's a scar the shape of a seahorse under her left eye, and one of her incisors is crooked, and her nails are bitten but very, very clean. We've worked together for a few months now, shared jokes about our sexist boss, and bonded during sneaky smoke breaks amongst the pig bins and milk crates, and now we're here, together, and she said she's enjoying herself.

I'm not a gamer but I'm working out how to level up: it's 1991 on the telly and Candi Staton's assuring me that I've Got the Love while Sam's gazing at me in a soft and misty kind of way. The pub's filled up so I've squeezed round the corner of the bench next to her, and the Zombie's already half-defeated. Sam reaches for her jacket.

"I need some fresh air," she says as she stands.

*

The bus shelter outside smells of wee but the patchwork of peeling posters and street lights diffused through scratched Perspex make for an almost romantic ambience.

"I like you," Sam says, reaching for my arm. She leans closer, and I remind myself to keep breathing as she grabs my forearm. Then she bends over my lap and vomits all over the dead leaves and my favourite trainers.

It takes a few minutes for all the cocktails to exit Sam's system. I hold her hair back as tenderly as I can in the circumstances, and comfort her with a crumpled tissue and half a stick of Wrigley's spearmint I've found in my pocket. Imagining her as a damsel in distress feels decidedly un-feminist, but I try to muster up an air of gender-neutral Knight in Shining Armour. Sam's smiling at me, and telling me I'm sweet, and apologising.

"It's fine," I tell her, "I'm feeling a bit wobbly myself."

Sam groans. "I hate puking, always makes me cry and feel pathetic. Ugh. I'm really sorry. I've ruined our night, haven't I?"

The pub doors swing open and I can hear The Wonder Stuff pondering the Size of a Cow. I'm not quite sure how to feel about any of this. Sam's talking about finding a taxi, and I'm trying to reassure her that everything's fine while wondering how to get the smell of vomit off my pumps.

"We can do it another time, honestly," I tell her. "We'll be laughing about it on Monday; as first dates go, it's a pretty good story."

Sam's edges are less blurry now, and my warm fuzzy feelings seem starkly delineated all of sudden. She looks confused.

"Wait," she says. "This was a DATE? I thought we were just going out on the lash. Oh God, I'm really sorry - I mean I really like you, I do, but not like THAT, you know? You're great, you really are, but… oh shit. I'm just not, well… *you know*?" and she pulls a grimace and wobbles her head which, unbeknown to me, must be the international gesture for *queer*.

She's checking her purse for change and glancing over my shoulder towards the taxi rank. I'm apologising too, and simmering with shame and nausea. I bluster my way through a jaunty no-harm-done goodnight, pull up my collar against the starting rain, and head for home.

I tap out my review on my phone as I drink a pint of water in bed, trying hard to be objective about a cocktail menu that's cost me both my dignity and a pair of nearly-new Converse All-Stars.

*

I wake up the next morning with a grotesque headache and a growing sense of mortification as the evening's events swim back into focus. Several coffees later a message from Sam lands on my phone, saying, *We're still mates, yes? PROMISE? X* and I try very hard to be philosophical about this.

I text her back: *Of COURSE* and spend far too long debating the semantics of the text-kiss with myself, eventually deciding on the same uppercase, singular X that Sam sent me, and then panicking again the moment I press 'Send'.

And that's that, really. Me and Sam see each other at work, and everything's fine. She even looks up how to clean pukey trainers on the internet, and they emerge from the washing machine devoid of any reminders of our night out. Without any awkward discussion whatsoever, Sam and I forge a tacit agreement to never, ever mention it again and nothing seems to be lost.

Well, I say 'nothing', but that's not strictly true. My itemised receipt says I spent £27.60 on two Mango Martinis, a pitcher of Planter's Punch, a fishbowl of Blue Meanie, and the jug of Zombie that I personally blame for the downwards turn in the evening's trajectory. I'm well within the thirty quid budget the mystery shopping agency set for me, but bizarrely my report and expenses come back marked, STATUS: NOT APPROVED. It takes twenty minutes on the phone to them to work out the problem.

The call centre lady is pleasant and breezy. Eventually she says, "So you went on Friday the twenty-second, yes?" and I tell her that yes, I did.

"Riiiight," she replies. "Well, we always advise our field researchers to check the brief carefully for the specifics of the visit -"

I interrupt her. "I did everything on the list: four different cocktails off the new menu. My - uh - friend and I drank them all."

"Yes," she agrees; "Your report is very thorough, but the trouble is, you went on the Friday - it should have been Saturday. We can't reimburse you because you went on the wrong date."

Sin Girls
by Emma Lloyd

Not the comfort of strangers
but rather
the sweet relief that comes
with the knowledge that
the chase is done.
Cell memory programmed
to respond to the known
and the knowing;
the shock of the new
confined to your lipstick:
Gay Geranium, you said,
as I kissed off its waxy vanilla.

Tobacco and hairspray
and a breath of *Soir de Paris*
as we hit the candlewick
and your petticoats crackle.

You're crying for God
and yet
they call it a sin.

Boil Wash
by Martagon

When life requires a boil wash
And all fibres ooze filth & grime
When morbid stains embed collar & cuff
It's enough

Act now whilst there's still time.

When acid sharp odours from a lifetime's toil
Cause frantic Bluebottles to hover
Above a festering laundry mountain
Of domesticity with my lover

When the ulcerating pile begs for brave Oxi-white
To rescue surfaces long dank and dirty
Instead of selecting 90°
The reluctant dial fixes tight:
On another wash of 30 @ 30

Difficult Windows
by Carole Powell

There is that smile. Again. The one
they share. That no one else knows.

The glass-blower says, *'The most
difficult colour to make
is the red.'* She turns and turns the glass.
It cools. And when it's molten again, uncurls.
All the reds shifted now
across a single flat plane.
None of them the same.
Each one different.

Like the smile. Un-
fathomable. All those deep reds.

And each section of the huge window
painstakingly created. The reds
floating there.
All the other colours
fizz and billow.
Greens. White.
The wild branches.
Have you seen the thorns?

-->

And this window, they say.
At every moment of every day

turns the light, turns it
to difference. Such wild colours on the walls
of each sunlit or unsunlit moment
registered there.
And the lines of people come
every day and stare. *'So why...? What do you...?
How...? Didn't you……? This
is all so different.'*

Like the smile.
The difficult reds.

how things are
by Carole Powell

that red Mazda you once had
won't be in regular internet range

and you can't trust taxi drivers
not wandering around at night

I think Russia is better
here I feel constantly on edge

towers guarding the bridge
some kind of laser show

flying through the night
just in different directions

a piece of clothing caught on a wire
an underground swimming pool

I read about the storm
heavy trucks stranded on the narrow streets

the churches closed
all the trains cancelled

smoke-rings
by Carole Powell

leaning on the grey bark
two of them   two trees

leaning there together   apart
smoke-rings in the moonfrost

somewhere far off   galloping
here in the stillmoon opening

white cotton bindings
unravelling   ravelling

and underneath   underneath
neither of them knowing

(the galloping still somewhere far off)
singing   faint at first

as if from inside   inside glass
and somehow infinitesimally unwinding

all the travelling   travelling
the long paths of the future

the two of them   leaning there
moonfrost and grey bark

the two of them   vessels
ringing   ringing

Through the Glass
by Carole Powell

Triangulated in the light
she slides at some invisible task.
Disappears behind the film. Over time
reappears. A bedroom. A living room.
A touch of indefinable colour in the black
and white sprung space, half-obscured
by rain-carried dust. Piano keys
halted under piles of archived manuscripts.
Through the glass, no one hears the words.

Along the front, between the ebbed sea and
cut black kaleidoscopic rock. A twisted
white swan. A crowd of silent
children. Pictures
taken. Pictures kept. Pictures
darken. Over time. In a pocket. In a cardboard box.
In a corner. In a cupboard. Even
on a shelf in a frame. Undisturbed.
Through the glass, no one hears.

Behind the heavy curtains, shadows.
Phantasmagoric space.
Across the slit of light
over time, a gull. Numbers
on a rusted registration plate. A single
shoe. Something spills
along the kerb. Clouds
a slash of horizontal curd.
Through the glass, no one.

A void …
by Paul Raven

TV news inflames his ire
He craves the daily protest,
'This Country's gone to Bloody Hell'.
Acidic broken record,
Long set mind set.

Militant old world bugger
Modern world reject.
Lost in vile rote memories
Of when Britain was perfect.

Neighbours long distant.
No visitors call.
Empty hearted bitter drinker
Now lives on the Darknet
… Fuels a dangerous audience
Beyond anonymous walls.

Growing Tomatoes
by Paul Raven

Money Maker takes six weeks
From seed to healthy fruit
Whilst a greenfingered wordsmith
Prunes off the wonky shoots

Nurtured by green cake and tea
Protective warmth and evening sun
Fertilised with kind words and similes
Until the gardener's job is done

Waiting & Watching
by Paul Raven

Waiting

Awake after midnight. Watching bad TV.
Waiting for life to happen to me.
A rented room in a poor London flat.
Cloying librarian flatmate asleep, at last.
Movie ends. The room now in darkness.
Reveals a watching stranger
Waiting at the uncurtained window.

Watching

2am. A still, black Kennington night.
The dog is waiting. A jacket is needed.
The walker fixes the lead and they exit.
The route is well trodden.
Their ritual begins.

As usual they pass no-one. Away from the street lights the silent shadows protect them.
The dog instinctively turns as they reach the housing complex.
The walker quickly scans the building and finds the uncurtained ground-floor window he is seeking.
They take up position across the narrow street.
The dog rests.

Flickering light from a TV reveals the unclothed male figure curled in an armchair.
The lousy room is sparsely furnished: A threadbare sofa, an unshaded floor lamp, a cheap junk shop bookcase.
A late night film noir holds the young man's attention and the walker is unnoticed.

Time passes.
They watch.

Each casual stretch and change of position reveals fresh milk smooth skin in the TV's blue light.
The walker is lost in dog-witnessed extacy.
The young man reaches for the remote, sinking the room into darkness.
Suddenly bereft, the walker moves to the now-black window, revealing himself for the first time.
Raising an arm he beckons to the young man: Come outside.

The young man retreats into the shadows,
He stares back at the watcher, unnerved but curious.
Aware of his nakedness.
The watcher holds his nerve ...
Waiting.

Gravitate
by Ren Williams

"Is gaydar really a thing?" Cooper asks.

I shrug. I don't know. I've never really thought so. It's something off the telly. I shift a little and settle further into my seat on the wall. I've found a flat stone to sit on and so has Cooper. The wall is newer than the church and the graveyard but still pretty old. It's stable though, enough for us at least.

Everything's quiet out here, even the spring lambs.

"What about transdar?"

Except Cooper of course.

The sleeping sheep in the field behind us grumble.

"Transdar?" I repeat, trying not to laugh.

"Yeah, gaydar but with trans people."

I sometimes regret coming out to Cooper. I should've known he'd have questions; he has questions about everything. A weird obsession with information. It's harmless mostly, I like that he wants to learn but it's tiring and Google exists.

"We sort of gravitate towards each other," I say eventually.

"Like magnets?"

"Gay magnets," I tell him with a smile.

He chuckles.

"Do you have a deadname?"

Okay, so he has been on the internet.

"That's mostly just trans people."

He nods and I wonder what he does with all this information he gathers. It's not like he's writing a book.

We're waiting for Myra. It's been an hour and it'll probably be an hour more. I can hear the crying start up though so maybe not quite that long.

"Animals can be gay too right? Saw that on facebook?"

I want to tell him he shouldn't believe everything he reads online but he's not wrong. Or did I read that online too?

"Am I the only gay person you know?" I ask instead.

It has dominated most of our conversations over the last two months, but it's a small village and few of us about these days.

We all fade away eventually. Like queer people, Cooper and I have gravitated towards each other. Alone, young, accident victims.

Not much else in common but what else is there?

Someone's hyperventilating, I can tell from here. It's not the first funeral we've attended and it won't be the last.

Like I said, we gravitate.

"I think so," he replies.

He probably doesn't even know many other people any more. The rest of the village is elderly. Only me and him are even under forty. Perhaps that's why he's trying to learn so much now; because he didn't before.

"What about you?"

"A few."

I live in a village surrounded by other villages. The kind of place where they have a WI and you're not supposed to go to the other village shows unless you're a spy. I always went along with it without question, like with most things. Explains how I ended up here certainly.

Cooper stands, stretches his legs. The hymns start again.

We don't sing.

I did once, Mrs Keystone's funeral. My voice didn't sound right, still doesn't even when I talk. I don't know about Cooper.

"What's your first name?" I ask.

It's been six months since we met, on this same stone wall outside this same stone church. He already knew my name and just introduced himself as Cooper and nothing else really mattered. Still doesn't I suppose but it would be nice to know.

Mrs Jones is wailing.

I don't blame her.

Cooper waits until someone consoles her, calms her, before he answers.

"Gwilym," he admits, "Cooper's cooler. Not that it's important now of course but it used to be. Plus there were three other Gwilyms in my year at school."

"Cooper is cooler," I agree.

The hymns are over, I can tell because the crying has started in earnest again. Or perhaps it's no longer drowned out by the organist. People are standing, pews are creaking – though usually at one of these it's bones too – and I slip off the wall to my feet.

A few minutes later and Father Justin walks out of the church, followed by the pallbearers carrying the coffin and a mass of black behind them.

Myra appears next to me, and I give her a weak smile. She's still adjusting, reconciling, so I wait.

Cooper doesn't.

"Welcome to the afterlife," he says cheerfully.

After the procession passes us by; Myra's mother held up by her brothers, I see the realisation on her face as she feels it.

"You're my welcoming committee?" she asks.

"Something like that," I reply.

She nods, watching her dad collapse to the grass.

"Thanks," she mutters.

Mewling Quim
by Ren Williams

Words we found
in secret or surprise
learning something new
that you shouldn't know.

At least not yet.

So they say.

I have come across words
in fiction and frank discussion
hidden them within until
I am able to decipher their meaning.

And,
a whole new world opens up
even now
I find new words,
slang, insults and supposition.

We've not fallen behind
nor are we lost
but we are found
in descriptors
only a dictionary can explain,

cause you sure as hell aren't going to ask anyone.

The Proper Biological Terms
by Ren Williams

Experts say
use the real names
but have you ever tried
to stop a toddler
shouting 'penis!' in a supermarket,
some would say willy and fanny
are a little easier to digest
in the dairy section.
No one wants to be that mum
but me I suppose.

Though regular use of words
and ownership
can take their power
you're still going to turn red
when your kid is telling you
their vagina is itchy
in the middle of the bank.
The real names they say,
any names I say
as long as we're all on the same page.